2016 SQA Past Papers With Answers

National 5
LIFESKILLS MATHEMATICS

2014, 2015 & 2016 Exams

HODDER
GIBSON
AN HACHETTE UK COMPANY

This book contains the official SQA 2014, 2015 and 2016 Exams for National 5 Lifeskills Mathematics, with associated SQA-approved answers modified from the official marking instructions that accompany the paper.

In addition the book contains study skills advice. This advice has been specially commissioned by Hodder Gibson, and has been written by experienced senior teachers and examiners in line with the new National 5 syllabus and assessment outlines. This is not SQA material but has been devised to provide further guidance for National 5 examinations.

Hodder Gibson is grateful to the copyright holders, as credited on the final page of the Answer Section, for permission to use their material. Every effort has been made to trace the copyright holders and to obtain their permission for the use of copyright material. Hodder Gibson will be happy to receive information allowing us to rectify any error or omission in future editions.

Hachette UK's policy is to use papers that are natural, renewable and recyclable products and made from wood grown in sustainable forests. The logging and manufacturing processes are expected to conform to the environmental regulations of the country of origin.

Orders: please contact Bookpoint Ltd, 130 Park Drive, Milton Park, Abingdon, Oxon OX14 4SE. Telephone: (44) 01235 827720. Fax: (44) 01235 400454. Lines are open 9.00–5.00, Monday to Saturday, with a 24-hour message answering service. Visit our website at www.hoddereducation.co.uk. Hodder Gibson can be contacted direct on: Tel: 0141 333 4650; Fax: 0141 404 8188; email: hoddergibson@hodder.co.uk

This collection first published in 2016 by
Hodder Gibson, an imprint of Hodder Education,
An Hachette UK Company
211 St Vincent Street
Glasgow G2 5QY

National 5 2014, 2015 and 2016 Exam Papers and Answers © Scottish Qualifications Authority. Study Skills section © Hodder Gibson. All rights reserved. Apart from any use permitted under UK copyright law, no part of this publication may be reproduced or transmitted in any form or by any means, electronic or mechanical, including photocopying and recording, or held within any information storage and retrieval system, without permission in writing from the publisher or under licence from the Copyright Licensing Agency Limited. Further details of such licences (for reprographic reproduction) may be obtained from the Copyright Licensing Agency Limited, Saffron House, 6–10 Kirby Street, London EC1N 8TS.

Typeset by Aptara, Inc.

Printed in the UK

A catalogue record for this title is available from the British Library

ISBN: 978-1-4718-9115-1

3 2 1

2017 2016

Introduction

Study Skills – what you need to know to pass exams!

Pause for thought

Many students might skip quickly through a page like this. After all, we all know how to revise. Do you really though?

Think about this:

"IF YOU ALWAYS DO WHAT YOU ALWAYS DO, YOU WILL ALWAYS GET WHAT YOU HAVE ALWAYS GOT."

Do you like the grades you get? Do you want to do better? If you get full marks in your assessment, then that's great! Change nothing! This section is just to help you get that little bit better than you already are.

There are two main parts to the advice on offer here. The first part highlights fairly obvious things but which are also very important. The second part makes suggestions about revision that you might not have thought about but which WILL help you.

Part 1

DOH! It's so obvious but …

Start revising in good time

Don't leave it until the last minute – this will make you panic.

Make a revision timetable that sets out work time AND play time.

Sleep and eat!

Obvious really, and very helpful. Avoid arguments or stressful things too – even games that wind you up. You need to be fit, awake and focused!

Know your place!

Make sure you know exactly **WHEN and WHERE** your exams are.

Know your enemy!

Make sure you know what to expect in the exam.

How is the paper structured?

How much time is there for each question?

What types of question are involved?

Which topics seem to come up time and time again?

Which topics are your strongest and which are your weakest?

Are all topics compulsory or are there choices?

Learn by DOING!

There is no substitute for past papers and practice papers – they are simply essential! Tackling this collection of papers and answers is exactly the right thing to be doing as your exams approach.

Part 2

People learn in different ways. Some like low light, some bright. Some like early morning, some like evening / night. Some prefer warm, some prefer cold. But everyone uses their BRAIN and the brain works when it is active. Passive learning – sitting gazing at notes – is the most INEFFICIENT way to learn anything. Below you will find tips and ideas for making your revision more effective and maybe even more enjoyable. What follows gets your brain active, and active learning works!

Activity 1 – Stop and review

Step 1

When you have done no more than 5 minutes of revision reading STOP!

Step 2

Write a heading in your own words which sums up the topic you have been revising.

Step 3

Write a summary of what you have revised in no more than two sentences. Don't fool yourself by saying, "I know it, but I cannot put it into words". That just means you don't know it well enough. If you cannot write your summary, revise that section again, knowing that you must write a summary at the end of it. Many of you will have notebooks full of blue/black ink writing. Many of the pages will not be especially attractive or memorable so try to liven them up a bit with colour as you are reviewing and rewriting. **This is a great memory aid, and memory is the most important thing.**

Activity 2 – Use technology!

Why should everything be written down? Have you thought about "mental" maps, diagrams, cartoons and colour to help you learn? And rather than write down notes, why not record your revision material?

What about having a text message revision session with friends? Keep in touch with them to find out how and what they are revising and share ideas and questions.

Why not make a video diary where you tell the camera what you are doing, what you think you have learned and what you still have to do? No one has to see or hear it, but the process of having to organise your thoughts in a formal way to explain something is a very important learning practice.

Be sure to make use of electronic files. You could begin to summarise your class notes. Your typing might be slow, but it will get faster and the typed notes will be easier to read than the scribbles in your class notes. Try to add different fonts and colours to make your work stand out. You can easily Google relevant pictures, cartoons and diagrams which you can copy and paste to make your work more attractive and **MEMORABLE**.

Activity 3 – This is it. Do this and you will know lots!

Step 1

In this task you must be very honest with yourself! Find the SQA syllabus for your subject (www.sqa.org.uk). Look at how it is broken down into main topics called MANDATORY knowledge. That means stuff you MUST know.

Step 2

BEFORE you do ANY revision on this topic, write a list of everything that you already know about the subject. It might be quite a long list but you only need to write it once. It shows you all the information that is already in your long-term memory so you know what parts you do not need to revise!

Step 3

Pick a chapter or section from your book or revision notes. Choose a fairly large section or a whole chapter to get the most out of this activity.

With a buddy, use Skype, Facetime, Twitter or any other communication you have, to play the game "If this is the answer, what is the question?". For example, if you are revising Geography and the answer you provide is "meander", your buddy would have to make up a question like "What is the word that describes a feature of a river where it flows slowly and bends often from side to side?".

Make up 10 "answers" based on the content of the chapter or section you are using. Give this to your buddy to solve while you solve theirs.

Step 4

Construct a wordsearch of at least 10 × 10 squares. You can make it as big as you like but keep it realistic. Work together with a group of friends. Many apps allow you to make wordsearch puzzles online. The words and phrases can go in any direction and phrases can be split. Your puzzle must only contain facts linked to the topic you are revising. Your task is to find 10 bits of information to hide in your puzzle, but you must not repeat information that you used in Step 3. DO NOT show where the words are. Fill up empty squares with random letters. Remember to keep a note of where your answers are hidden but do not show your friends. When you have a complete puzzle, exchange it with a friend to solve each other's puzzle.

Step 5

Now make up 10 questions (not "answers" this time) based on the same chapter used in the previous two tasks. Again, you must find NEW information that you have not yet used. Now it's getting hard to find that new information! Again, give your questions to a friend to answer.

Step 6

As you have been doing the puzzles, your brain has been actively searching for new information. Now write a NEW LIST that contains only the new information you have discovered when doing the puzzles. Your new list is the one to look at repeatedly for short bursts over the next few days. Try to remember more and more of it without looking at it. After a few days, you should be able to add words from your second list to your first list as you increase the information in your long-term memory.

FINALLY! Be inspired...

Make a list of different revision ideas and beside each one write **THINGS I HAVE** tried, **THINGS I WILL** try and **THINGS I MIGHT** try. Don't be scared of trying something new.

And remember – "FAIL TO PREPARE AND PREPARE TO FAIL!"

National 5 Lifeskills Mathematics

The course

The Lifeskills Mathematics course is a new qualification which focuses on the application of mathematical skills in real-life contexts.

The National 5 Lifeskills Mathematics course aims to enable you to develop:

- a range of mathematical techniques and apply these to real-life problems or situations
- the ability to analyse a range of real-life problems or situations
- a confident and independent approach towards the use of mathematics in real-life situations
- the ability to select, apply and combine mathematical skills to new or unfamiliar situations in life and work
- the ability to use mathematical reasoning skills to generalise, support arguments, draw conclusions, assess risk and make informed decisions
- the ability to analyse, interpret and present a range of information
- the ability to communicate mathematical information in a variety of forms
- the ability to think creatively and in abstract ways.

Before starting this course you should already have the knowledge, understanding and skills required to achieve a pass in National 4 Lifeskills Mathematics and/or be proficient in appropriate experiences and outcomes.

This course enables you to further develop your knowledge, understanding, skills and reasoning processes in personal finance, statistics, geometry, measure, numeracy and data. The table outlines the topics covered in each area of the course:

Finance	Statistics	Numeracy
Budgeting	Investigate probability/risk	Select and use appropriate
Income and pay slips	Statistical diagrams	notation and units
Tax and deductions	Analyse/compare data sets	Select and carry out operations
Best deal	Line of best fit	including:
Currency conversion		• working to given decimal places
Interest rates and saving/borrowing		• rounding to given significant figures
Geometry	**Graphical Data**	• fractions and mixed numbers
Gradient	Extract/interpret data	• percentages, including compound
Composite shapes: Area	from at least three different	• speed, distance, time
Composite solids: Volume	graphical forms	• area
Pythagoras' theorem	Make/justify decisions based	• volume
Measure	on interpretation of data	• ratio
Scale drawing	Make/justify decisions based	• proportion, direct and indirect
Bearings	on probability	
Container packing		
Precedence tables		
Time management		
Tolerance		

You will use your reasoning skills and the skills above, linked to real-life contexts. The amount of reasoning is what makes Lifeskills Mathematics different. You will be asked to analyse, compare, justify and communicate information.

Assessment

To gain the course award, you must pass the three Units – Managing Finance and Statistics, Geometry and Measures and Numeracy and Data – as well as the examination. The Units are assessed internally on a pass/fail basis and the examination is set and marked externally by SQA. It tests skills beyond the minimum competence required for the Units.

The number of marks and the times allotted for the examination papers are as follows:

| Paper 1 (non-calculator) | 35 marks | 50 minutes |
| Paper 2 | 55 marks | 1 hour 40 minutes |

The course award is graded A–D, the grade being determined by the total mark you score in the examination.

The papers are "structured" which means that you write your answer on the exam paper next to the question. This gives you the advantage of being able to complete tables, draw on graphs and annotate diagrams, without having to draw them yourself.

Some tips for achieving a good mark

- **DOING** maths questions is the most effective use of your study time. You will benefit much more from spending 30 minutes doing maths questions than spending several hours copying out notes or reading a maths textbook.

- Practise doing the types of questions that are likely to appear in the exam. Use the marking instructions to check your answers and to understand what the examiners are looking for. Ask your teacher for help if you get stuck.

- **SHOW ALL WORKING CLEARLY.** The instructions on the front of the exam paper state that *"Full credit will only be given where the solution contains appropriate working"*. A "correct" answer with no working may only be awarded partial marks or even no marks at all. An incomplete answer will be awarded marks for any appropriate working. Attempt every question, even if you are not sure whether you are correct or not. Your solution may contain working which will gain some marks. A blank response is certain to be awarded no marks. Never score out working unless you have something better to replace it with.

- Reasoning skills are a major part of Lifeskills Mathematics. One way of showing your reasoning process is by showing all of your working. Quite often you will be asked to *"Use your working to justify your answer"* – so you cannot just say "yes" or "no" without your working.

- Communication is very important in presenting solutions to questions. Diagrams are often a good way of conveying information and enabling markers to understand your working. Where a diagram is included in a question, it is often good practice to mark in any dimensions etc, which you work out and may use later.

- In Paper 1, you have to carry out calculations without a calculator. Ensure that you practise your number skills regularly, especially within questions that test course content. Also make sure that after you have calculated an answer you state the **units**, if appropriate. Paper 1 will be a mixture of short, medium and extended questions covering a single "skill", to three or four skills across the Units.

- In Paper 2, you will be allowed to use a calculator. Always use **your own** calculator. Different calculators often function in slightly different ways, so make sure that you know how to operate yours. Having to use a calculator that you are unfamiliar with on the day of the exam may cause frustration and loss of time. Paper 2 will be a mixture of short, medium and extended **case studies**. These will follow a "theme" and can cover one skill within a Unit to three or more from across the Units.

- Prepare thoroughly to tackle questions from **all** parts of the course. Always try all parts of a question. Just because you could not complete part (a), for example, this does not mean you could not do part (b) or (c).

- Look at how many **marks** are allocated to a question – this will give you an idea of how much work is required. The more marks, the more work!

- Look for **key words** in questions: state, calculate, compare, plot, sketch, draw, justify.

Some areas to consider

Each question is likely to have a mixture of strategy, process and communication marks.

You will be expected to:

- select a strategy (there may be more than one way to do a question)
- process the information (for example, carry out a calculation)
- communicate your answer (for example, "yes the company would accept as tolerance is within limits").

Here are some examples to consider:

Types of question	Things to consider
You may be asked to mark points on a scatter diagram, draw a line of best fit and then compare it with one already drawn.	Ensure points are **plotted accurately**. Try to make the **"slope"** of the line match points. Try to have about same number of points above and below the line of best fit.
You may be asked to make a scale drawing of, for example, a garden. You may then be asked to calculate measurements from this drawing.	Choose a scale which gives a good size, to fit the space given to you. **State the scale** you have used. Use this scale to calculate actual sizes. Remember to **state units**.
You may be asked to construct a box plot. You may have to compare this with one given.	Make sure you have a scale clearly marked. Make sure you mark in the **five-figure summary**. Valid comparison: 1 mark equals one comparison, 2 marks equal two comparison statements. For example, "plot 2 has a higher median and a greater spread".

In Paper 2 you have been given more time to allow you to read and absorb the information given.

Use the first one or two case studies to get "into the swing of it". These will be short case studies looking at perhaps only one skill, for example, from Managing Finance and Statistics you may be tasked to complete a payslip. Take your time and complete these accurately – this could be a 5 mark start to the paper!

You may be asked to calculate the standard deviation for a set of data. Again, take your time and do this accurately. These are "processing" questions and should allow you a "cushion" before you put your reasoning into place for later case studies.

A medium-length case study will cover areas such as speed, distance, time along with money. For example, "what will be the cost of fuel for a journey given the data on distance, speed, fuel consumption?" and so on. An extended case study will perhaps cover skills from across all three Units. For example, from Working to a Budget, "could you plan a holiday taking in three different places, with certain likely temperatures over a period of time, staying in the cheapest hotels and travelling by train?"

In Paper 2 you should not have to "turn pages" between information and questions. If it is a short case study, there will be space on one page. If it is a longer case study, the information will be on the left-hand page and the questions on the right-hand side, as in the diagram below.

Left-hand page	Right-hand page
Table of information	Question 1a
Statements of information	Question 1b
Facts and figures	Question 1 c
Graphs or diagrams	

Look through these past papers to get a feel for the type and variety of questions you could be asked.

Remember that Lifeskills Mathematics is all about analysing, interpreting, solving, justifying and communicating!

Good luck!

Remember that the rewards for passing National 5 Lifeskills Mathematics are well worth it! Your pass will help you get the future you want for yourself. In the exam, be confident in your own ability. If you're not sure how to answer a question, trust your instincts and just give it a go anyway. Keep calm and don't panic! GOOD LUCK!

NATIONAL 5

2014

National Qualifications 2014

Mark

X744/75/01

**Lifeskills Mathematics
Paper 1
(Non-Calculator)**

FRIDAY, 9 MAY
1:00 PM – 1:50 PM

Fill in these boxes and read what is printed below.

Full name of centre

Town

Forename(s)

Surname

Number of seat

Date of birth

Day	Month	Year
D D	M M	Y Y

Scottish candidate number

Total marks — 35

Attempt ALL questions.

Write your answers in the spaces provided in this booklet. Additional space for answers is provided at the end of this booklet. If you use this space you must clearly identify question number you are attempting.

Use **blue** or **black** ink.

You may NOT use a calculator.

Full credit will be given only to solutions which contain appropriate working.

State the units for your answer where appropriate.

Before leaving the examination room you must give this booklet to the Invigilator; if you do not, you may lose all the marks for this paper.

FORMULAE LIST

Circumference of a circle: $C = \pi d$

Area of a circle: $A = \pi r^2$

Theorem of Pythagoras:

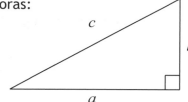

$$a^2 + b^2 = c^2$$

Volume of a cylinder: $V = \pi r^2 h$

Volume of a prism: $V = Ah$

Volume of a cone: $V = \frac{1}{3}\pi r^2 h$

Volume of a sphere: $V = \frac{4}{3}\pi r^3$

Standard deviation: $s = \sqrt{\dfrac{\Sigma(x-\bar{x})^2}{n-1}} = \sqrt{\dfrac{\Sigma x^2 - (\Sigma x)^2/n}{n-1}}$, where n is the sample size.

Gradient:

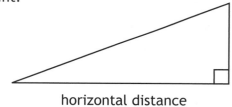

$$\text{gradient} = \frac{\text{vertical height}}{\text{horizontal distance}}$$

MARKS

Attempt ALL questions

1. Mrs Abid took a survey in her mathematics class of how pupils travelled to school.

   The results are shown in the table.

	Walk	Cycle	Bus
Boys	6	4	3
Girls	2	3	12

   What is the probability that a pupil chosen at random is a girl who cycles to school?

   Give your answer in its simplest form.   2

   [Turn over

MARKS | DO NOT WRITE IN THIS MARGIN

2. Frances is not feeling well.

She takes her temperature using a thermometer.

Her temperature is shown below.

The temperature of a person in good health is $36 \cdot 8°C \pm 0 \cdot 4°C$.

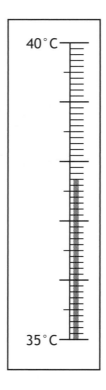

Is Frances in good health?

Give a reason for your answer.   3

MARKS | DO NOT WRITE IN THIS MARGIN

3. A new sail is being designed for a yacht as shown below.

It consists of two right angled triangles.

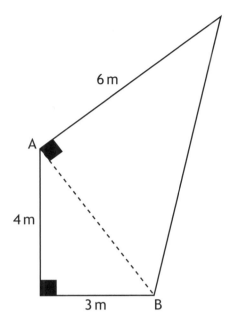

(a) Calculate the length of AB.   1

(b) Calculate the total area of the sail.   2

Total marks   3

[Turn over

MARKS | DO NOT WRITE IN THIS MARGIN

4. Adam works for 40 hours per week as a tractor driver on a farm.

   His basic wage is £7·40 per hour.

   Each week he pays £28·43 Income Tax and £8·57 in National Insurance.

   (a) Calculate his take home pay.

   1

MARKS | DO NOT WRITE IN THIS MARGIN

4. **(continued)**

(b) Adam is going on holiday in 13 weeks.

The holiday costs £320 and Adam wants to take £200 spending money.

He makes a table to show his weekly income and outgoings.

He puts the balance into his holiday fund.

	Income	Outgoings
Take home pay		
Rent		£76
Bills		£41
Food		£45
Entertainment		£30
Transport		£23
Holiday Fund		

Will he have enough to cover the cost of the holiday and his spending money?

Justify your answer.

3

Total marks   4

[Turn over

MARKS

DO NOT WRITE IN THIS MARGIN

5. Reece is given a lift to school.

She leaves the house at 8:30 am and arrives at school at 8:50 am.

She uses an app on her phone to calculate her average speed for the journey.

Her phone displays 6·8m/s.

What distance did she travel?

Give your answer to 2 significant figures.

4

6. The Clarks employ Kitease to install a new kitchen for them.

    Kitease provide a team of workers to install the kitchen.

    The table shows the list of tasks and the time required for each.

Task	Detail	Preceding task	Time(hours)
A	Begin electrics	None	3
B	Build cupboards	None	5
C	Begin plumbing	None	2
D	Plaster walls	A,B,C	8
E	Fit wall cupboards	D	6
F	Fit floor cupboards	D	5
G	Fit worktops	F	3
H	Finish plumbing	G	3
I	Finish electrics	E,G	4

(a) Complete the diagram below by writing these tasks and times in the boxes.

   (An additional diagram, if required, can be found on *Page fifteen*.)

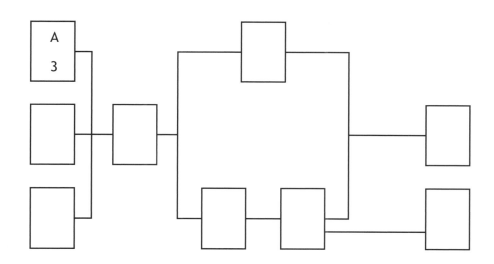

2

(b) Kitease claim they can install this kitchen in 22 hours.

   Is this a valid claim?

   Give a reason for your answer.   2

Total marks   4

[Turn over

7. This back-to-back stem and leaf diagram represents the number of hours a class spends on social networking websites in a week.

```
         Girls |   | Boys
               | 0 | 3 6 8 9
       8 4 3 0 | 1 | 1 2 4 7 7 8 9
 9 8 7 6 2 2 1 | 2 | 2 6 7 8 8
         7 2 0 | 3 |
             2 | 4 |
```

n = 15   n = 16

KEY

```
3 | 1 |     represents 13 hours
  | 2 | 5   represents 25 hours
```

(a) A boxplot is drawn to represent one set of data.

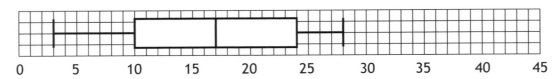

0   5   10   15   20   25   30   35   40   45

Which set of data does this represent?

Give a reason for your answer.   1

MARKS

7.　(continued)

(b)　For the other set of data, state:

the median

the lower quartile

the upper quartile　　　　2

(c)　Construct a box plot for the second set of data.

(An additional diagram, if required, can be found on *Page fifteen*.)

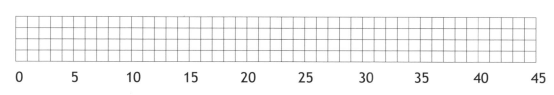

0　　5　　10　　15　　20　　25　　30　　35　　40　　45

2

Total marks　5

[Turn over

MARKS | DO NOT WRITE IN THIS MARGIN

8. Elaine goes on a 5 day long business trip to Oslo in Norway.

    She changes £750 to Norwegian kroner for the trip.

Rates of exchange	
Pounds Sterling (£)	Other Currencies
1	NOK 8·00 (Norwegian kroner)
1	€1·20 (euros)

(a) How many Norwegian kroner will Elaine receive?   1

MARKS

8. (continued)

   (b)   Elaine spends NOK 520 each day she is in Norway.

       Her company extends her trip by sending her to Munich in Germany for a further 3 days.

       If she changes all her remaining kroner to euros, how many euros will she receive?

       She spends €135 each day she is in Munich.

       How much money does she have left at the end of her trip?

       Give your answer in pounds sterling.   5

Total marks   6

[Turn over for Question 9 on *Page Fourteen*

MARKS | DO NOT WRITE IN THIS MARGIN

9. Robbie has a tub for his crayons.

   It is in the shape of a pencil as shown below.

   It consists of a cylinder with a cone on top.

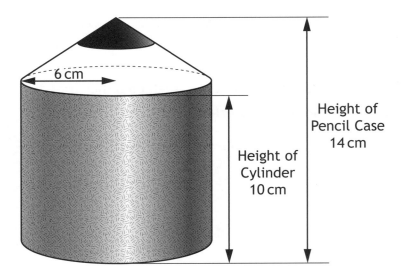

6 cm

Height of Pencil Case 14 cm

Height of Cylinder 10 cm

Show that the volume of Robbie's tub is $408\,\pi\ \text{cm}^3$.   **4**

[END OF QUESTION PAPER]

MARKS | DO NOT WRITE IN THIS MARGIN

ADDITIONAL SPACE FOR ANSWERS

Additional diagram for Question 6 (a)

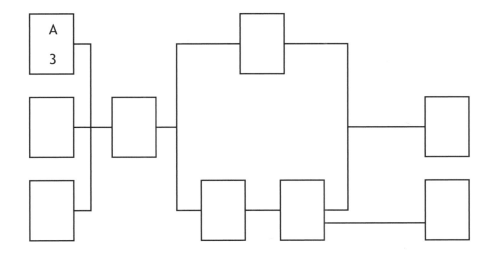

Additional diagram for Question 7 (c)

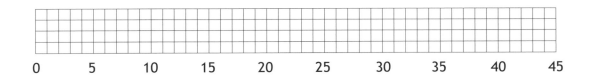

0   5   10   15   20   25   30   35   40   45

MARKS

ADDITIONAL SPACE FOR ANSWERS

FOR OFFICIAL USE

N5

National Qualifications 2014

Mark

X744/75/02

**Lifeskills Mathematics
Paper 2**

FRIDAY, 9 MAY
2:10 PM — 3:50 PM

Fill in these boxes and read what is printed below.

Full name of centre

Town

Forename(s)

Surname

Number of seat

Date of birth

Day	Month	Year
D D	M M	Y Y

Scottish candidate number

Total marks — 55

Attempt ALL questions.

Write your answers clearly in the spaces provided in this booklet. Additional space for answers is provided at the end of this booklet. If you use this space you must clearly identify the question number you are attempting.

Use **blue** or **black** ink.

You may use a calculator.

Full credit will be given only to solutions which contain appropriate working.

State the units for your answer where appropriate.

Before leaving the examination room you must give this booklet to the Invigilator; if you do not, you may lose all the marks for this paper.

FORMULAE LIST

Circumference of a circle: $C = \pi d$

Area of a circle: $A = \pi r^2$

Theorem of Pythagoras:

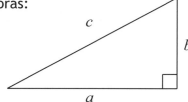

$$a^2 + b^2 = c^2$$

Volume of a cylinder: $V = \pi r^2 h$

Volume of a prism: $V = Ah$

Volume of a cone: $V = \frac{1}{3}\pi r^2 h$

Volume of a sphere: $V = \frac{4}{3}\pi r^3$

Standard deviation: $s = \sqrt{\dfrac{\Sigma(x - \bar{x})^2}{n-1}} = \sqrt{\dfrac{\Sigma x^2 - (\Sigma x)^2/n}{n-1}}$, where n is the sample size.

Gradient:

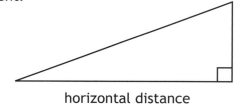

$$\text{gradient} = \frac{\text{vertical height}}{\text{horizontal distance}}$$

MARKS

Attempt ALL questions

1. Over an eight month period, Goran records how much he spends on his pay-as-you-go mobile phone.

   £32, £23, £43, £40, £27, £35, £15, £25.

   Calculate the mean and standard deviation for this data.   4

[Turn over

MARKS

2. The Yellow Jersey Cycle Shop is a retail store that sells items for outdoor activities.

Alan has a 10% discount card for this store.

He receives a flyer showing the store's monthly deals.

He wants to buy all of the following items.

	Mountain Bike Recommended Retail Price £310 Price with discount card £279
	Helmet Recommended Retail Price £20 Price with discount card £18
	Waterproof Jacket Recommended Retail Price £50 Price with discount card £45
	Cycling Shorts Recommended Retail Price £10 Price with discount card £9

Monthly Deal 1	**Monthly Deal 2**
Extra 15% off discounted price when you spend over £75 in store.	Extra 65% off discounted price of bike accessories and clothing when you purchase a bike in store.
Terms & Conditions. 1. Can be used in conjunction with 10% discount card. 2. Not to be used with any other offer or monthly deal. 3. Valid until end of May.	Terms & Conditions. 1. Can be used in conjunction with 10% discount card. 2. Not to be used with any other offer or monthly deal. 3. Valid until end of May.

MARKS

Question 2 (continued)

(a) Which Monthly Deal is better value for Alan?

Justify your answer.

3

(b) After he has bought the items Alan notices the following on his receipt.

> **The Yellow Jersey Cycle Shop**
> **Price Guarantee**
> If any product can be found cheaper (including on special offer) then we will refund the difference plus 10% of the difference.

Alan finds exactly the same items at The Red Polka Dot Cycle Shop who are having a clearance sale.

They are giving 1/3 off the Recommended Retail Price of all the items that Alan has just bought.

How much refund is he entitled to if he uses the **Price Guarantee** from The Yellow Jersey Cycle Shop?

3

Total marks   6

[Turn over

MARKS

3. A number of oil rigs operate in the North Sea.

The map below shows part of the North Sea with the ports of Aberdeen and Ringkobing marked.

(An additional map, if required, can be found on *Page fourteen*.)

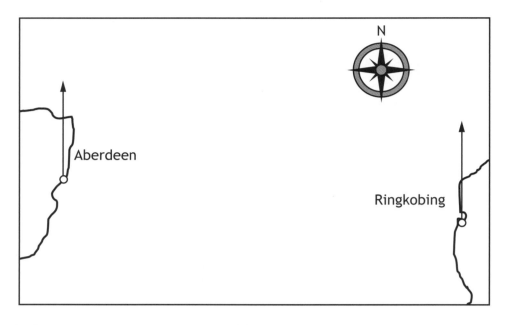

Scale 1 centimetre represents 50 kilometres

(a) Harkins oil rig is 380 km from Aberdeen on a bearing of 065°.

   Show the position of the Harkins oil rig on the map above.   2

(b) A fishing vessel issues an SOS call which is received by both ports.

   The bearing of the fishing vessel from each port is shown in the table below.

Bearing from	Three figure bearing
Aberdeen	125°
Ringkobing	250°

   (i) Mark the position of the fishing vessel on the map.   3

   (ii) Find the distance and bearing of the fishing vessel from the oil rig.   2

Total marks   7

MARKS

4. Saraish bought her house in May 2009 for £130 000.

In the first two years the value of the house increased by 5% per annum.

For the next three years the value of the house decreased by 2% per annum.

(a) What is the value of the house in May 2014?

   Give your answer to the nearest thousand pounds.   5

(b) House prices have risen on average by 4·5% over this five year period.

   Has the value of Saraish's house risen in line with this average?

   Give a reason for your answer.   2

Total marks   7

[Turn over

MARKS

5. A landscape gardener is designing a garden.

The rectangular garden has dimensions 15 metres by 10 metres.

He plans to build a triangular flower bed.

To separate the flower bed from the lawn, he uses a low fence.

The fence is made of 5 sections, each 2·8 metres long.

A patio in the shape of a quarter circle with a radius of 5 metres is to be created in the corner.

The rest of the garden is to be laid as turf.

A sketch of the garden is shown below.

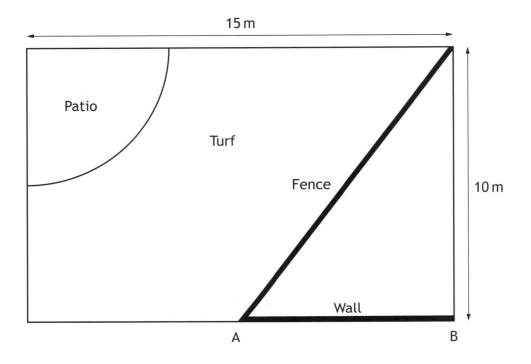

(a) Calculate the length of the wall, AB.   3

MARKS

5. **(continued)**

(b) Turf is sold in $5\,m^2$ rolls costing £14·95 per roll.

Calculate the cost of buying turf for this garden.   **6**

Total marks   9

[Turn over

6. The table shows the qualifying times at the Malaysian 2013 Grand Prix.

   The qualifying times are for 1 lap of the track.

   The track is 5·543 kilometres long.

   There are 56 laps in this Grand Prix.

	Driver	Team	Qualifying Time (min: sec)
1	Sebastian Vettel	Red Bull	01:49·7
2	Felipe Massa	Ferrari	01:50·6
3	Fernando Alonso	Ferrari	01:50·7
4	Lewis Hamilton	Mercedes	01:51·7
5	Mark Webber	Red Bull	01:52·2
6	Nico Rosberg	Mercedes	01:52·5

   (a) Vettel's time was 1 minute 49·7 seconds.

   By how much time did Vettel beat Massa?   **1**

   (b) What was Lewis Hamilton's average speed in his qualifying lap?

   Round your answer to the nearest km/h.   **5**

MARKS

6. **(continued)**

(c) Nico Rosberg's average lap time for the Grand Prix was 1 minute 54·8 seconds.

How long did it take him to complete the Grand Prix?

Give your answer in hours, minutes and seconds.   **4**

Total marks 10

[Turn over

MARKS | DO NOT WRITE IN THIS MARGIN

7. Cameron wants to resurface his drive.

He has a choice of 3 surfaces.

SURFACE TYPE 1: TARMAC
A tarmac drive should last for 30 years.

Tarmac costs £2 per square foot to lay.

(1 square metre = 10·76 square feet)

SURFACE TYPE 2: GRAVEL CHIPS
A gravel drive should last for 10 years.

Gravel needs to be laid to a depth of 5 cm.

Each 50 kg bag will cover 1 square metre to a depth of 5 cm.
Each 50 kg bag costs £8·29
Each 850 kg bag costs £125·99

The gravel needs a weedproof membrane to be laid underneath.
Membrane to cover the drive costs £14·31.

SURFACE TYPE 3: CONCRETE SLABS
A concrete slab drive should last for 25 years.

Concrete slabs:
40 cm by 40 cm ------------ £2·12 each
Slabs can be cut to size

Slabs require 4 cm depth of hardcore to be laid underneath.
1 cubic metre = 2 tonnes hardcore.
Hardcore costs £18 per tonne bag.

2 bags of mortar at £35·99 per bag.

Cameron makes a sketch of his drive to help him to calculate the cost of each type of surface.

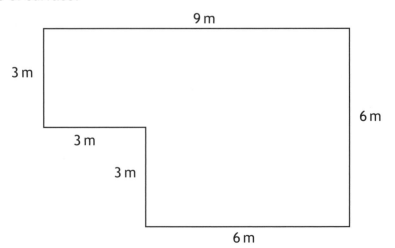

MARKS

7. **(continued)**

(a) Calculate the minimum total cost for each surface type.   9

(b) Which is the most cost effective?   3

Total marks 12

[END OF QUESTION PAPER]

MARKS | DO NOT WRITE IN THIS MARGIN

ADDITIONAL SPACE FOR ANSWERS

Additional map for Question 3

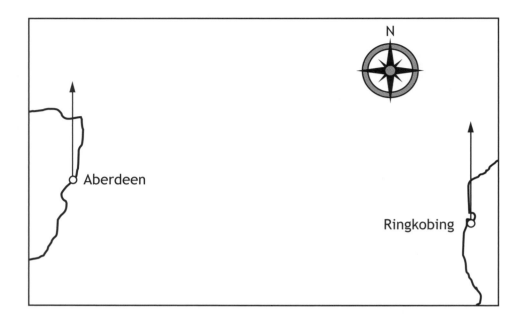

MARKS

ADDITIONAL SPACE FOR ANSWERS

[BLANK PAGE]

DO NOT WRITE ON THIS PAGE

NATIONAL 5

2015

FOR OFFICIAL USE

N5

National Qualifications 2015

Mark

X744/75/01

**Lifeskills Mathematics
Paper 1 (Non-Calculator)**

WEDNESDAY, 29 APRIL

1:00 PM – 1:50 PM

Fill in these boxes and read what is printed below.

Full name of centre

Town

Forename(s)

Surname

Number of seat

Date of birth

Day	Month	Year		Scottish candidate number

Total marks — 35

Attempt ALL questions.

Write your answers in the spaces provided in this booklet. Additional space for answers is provided at the end of this booklet. If you use this space you must clearly identify the question number you are attempting.

Use **blue** or **black** ink.

You may NOT use a calculator.

Full credit will be given only to solutions which contain appropriate working.

State the units for your answer where appropriate.

Before leaving the examination room you must give this booklet to the Invigilator; if you do not, you may lose all the marks for this paper.

FORMULAE LIST

Circumference of a circle: $C = \pi d$

Area of a circle: $A = \pi r^2$

Theorem of Pythagoras:

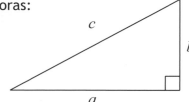

$$a^2 + b^2 = c^2$$

Volume of a cylinder: $V = \pi r^2 h$

Volume of a prism: $V = Ah$

Volume of a cone: $V = \frac{1}{3}\pi r^2 h$

Volume of a sphere: $V = \frac{4}{3}\pi r^3$

Standard deviation: $s = \sqrt{\dfrac{\Sigma(x - \bar{x})^2}{n-1}} = \sqrt{\dfrac{\Sigma x^2 - (\Sigma x)^2/n}{n-1}}$, where n is the sample size.

Gradient:

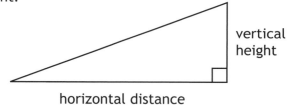

$$\text{gradient} = \frac{\text{vertical height}}{\text{horizontal distance}}$$

Total marks — 35

Attempt ALL questions

1. Carol knows that she can travel 280 miles on a full tank of fuel. She is making a trip of 110 miles.

   The diagram below shows the car's fuel gauge

   Full

   Empty

   Does she have enough fuel to make the journey?

   Show working to justify your answer.

   2

2. Usain flies from London to Moscow for a business meeting.

   The plane leaves London at 1845.

   The flight takes 3 hours and 40 minutes.

   Moscow time is 4 hours ahead of London.

   It should take 45 minutes to collect his luggage and clear security.

   His company arranges for a driver to collect him from Moscow Airport.

   At what time should the driver expect to collect Usain?

   2

[Turn over

3. Freddie and Kamal work in a warehouse stacking shelves.

A section of the warehouse has 5 shelves; each shelf is 10 metres in length.

The shelves are currently stocked as shown below.

Shelf 1	Box A (7 m)
Shelf 2	Box B (5 m)
Shelf 3	Box C (6 m) Box D (3 m)
Shelf 4	Box E (4 m) Box F (3 m)
Shelf 5	Box G (2 m)

A new delivery of Box H (6 m), Box I (5 m), Box J (3 m), Box K (4 m), Box L (1 m) arrives to be stored in this section of the warehouse.

These new boxes need to be stored on different shelves from the existing stock.

The existing stock can be re-arranged to create space for the new delivery.

By writing the letters A to L in the diagram below, show how Freddie and Kamal can fit **all** the boxes onto the shelves.

(An additional diagram, if required can be found on *Page eleven*)   2

Shelf 1	
Shelf 2	
Shelf 3	
Shelf 4	
Shelf 5	

MARKS | DO NOT WRITE IN THIS MARGIN

4. A company orders a batch of washers with a thickness of $2 \cdot 4 \pm 0 \cdot 05$ mm.

A quality control inspector takes a sample from the batch of washers.

The thicknesses, in mm, of the washers in this sample are shown below.

2·44, 2·37, 2·36, 2·45, 2·35

2·35, 2·44, 2·43, 2·34, 2·40

2·40, 2·41, 2·39, 2·38, 2·46

2·41, 2·39, 2·53, 2·36, 2·37

For the batch to be accepted, at least 88% of the washers in this sample must be within tolerance.

Will the batch be accepted?

3

5. A shop sells Ice Cola in 330 millilitre cans.

An individual can costs 66 pence.

Complete the shelf label for Ice Cola below to show the price per litre.

2

330 ml	equivalent to	1 litre
66p		_____

[Turn over

MARKS

6. Mhairi buys 200 shares for £700.

   When she decides to sell them, the share price has dropped to £2·75 per share.

   She has to pay a fee of 2½% of her selling price when she sells her shares.

   Calculate the loss that she has made. **4**

7. Lucy has a scarf in the shape of an isosceles triangle with dimensions as shown below.

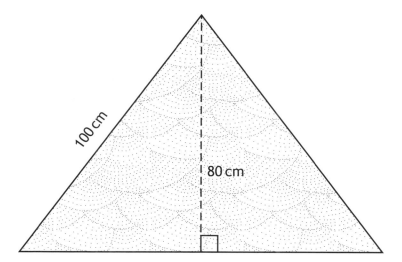

100 cm

80 cm

Lucy wants to sew ribbon along all three edges of the scarf.

She has 3·5 metres of ribbon.

Does Lucy have enough ribbon for the scarf?

Show all working and justify your answer.

4

[Turn over

MARKS | DO NOT WRITE IN THIS MARGIN

8. The diagram below shows a staircase Mark intends to install in his home.

The dimensions of the riser and tread of each step are shown.

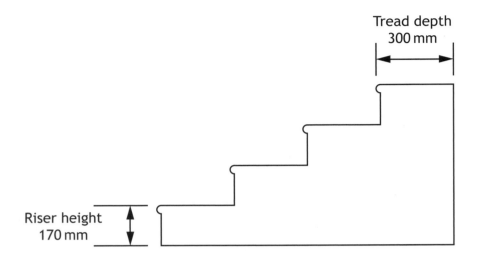

Tread depth
300 mm

Riser height
170 mm

For safety reasons, these rules must be applied.

- Twice the riser height plus the tread depth should be 625 mm ±15 mm.
- The gradient of each step should be less than ½.

Mark thinks that this staircase will meet both of these rules.

Is Mark correct?

Use your working to justify your answer.

5

MARKS | DO NOT WRITE IN THIS MARGIN

9. Novak is going to buy a new computer system. He researches online to find the prices from different retailers.

Retailer	Keyboard	Monitor	Computer Tower	Mouse	Printer
Easy Comp	50	130	130	15	95
ABC	45	135	140	20	75
Compact	30	125	180	25	120
Hardy's	70	130	165	15	125
Tonda	35	115	150	20	80
Disme	40	120	180	10	105

All prices are in £s

(a) Novak needs to buy one of each item. He is happy to buy these from different retailers.

What is the minimum total cost for his new computer system?   1

(b) Novak cannot afford to pay for his computer system all at once.

Disme can provide a finance package to buy the complete computer system.

The deposit is 10% of the cash price, followed by 12 payments of £40.

He chooses to buy the complete computer system from Disme using their finance package.

How much more than the minimum total will this cost him?   4

[Turn over

MARKS | DO NOT WRITE IN THIS MARGIN

10. A hotel is redecorating their function room which includes a semi-circular stage area.

They plan to lay a hardwood floor.

A sketch of the floor plan of the room is shown below.

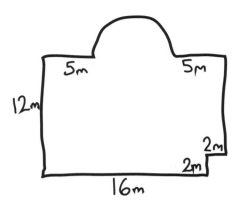

(a) Calculate the area of the floor in the hotel's function room.

   Use $\pi = 3\cdot14$. 4

(b) Hardwood flooring comes in packs of 4m² and is sold at £67·95 per pack.

   Calculate the cost for the hotel to floor their function room. 2

[END OF QUESTION PAPER]

ADDITIONAL SPACE FOR ANSWERS

Additional diagram for Question 3

Shelf 1	
Shelf 2	
Shelf 3	
Shelf 4	
Shelf 5	

MARKS

ADDITIONAL SPACE FOR ANSWERS

FOR OFFICIAL USE

N5

National Qualifications 2015

Mark

X744/75/02

Lifeskills Mathematics
Paper 2

WEDNESDAY, 29 APRIL

2:10 PM – 3:50 PM

Fill in these boxes and read what is printed below.

Full name of centre

Town

Forename(s)

Surname

Number of seat

Date of birth

Day   Month   Year

Scottish candidate number

Total marks — 55

Attempt ALL questions.

Write your answers clearly in the spaces provided in this booklet. Additional space for answers is provided at the end of this booklet. If you use this space you must clearly identify the question number you are attempting.

Use **blue** or **black** ink.

You may use a calculator.

Full credit will be given only to solutions which contain appropriate working.

State the units for your answer where appropriate.

Before leaving the examination room you must give this book to the Invigilator; if you do not, you may lose all the marks for this paper.

FORMULAE LIST

Circumference of a circle: $C = \pi d$

Area of a circle: $A = \pi r^2$

Theorem of Pythagoras:

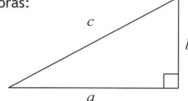

$$a^2 + b^2 = c^2$$

Volume of a cylinder: $V = \pi r^2 h$

Volume of a prism: $V = Ah$

Volume of a cone: $V = \frac{1}{3}\pi r^2 h$

Volume of a sphere: $V = \frac{4}{3}\pi r^3$

Standard deviation: $s = \sqrt{\dfrac{\Sigma(x - \bar{x})^2}{n-1}} = \sqrt{\dfrac{\Sigma x^2 - (\Sigma x)^2/n}{n-1}}$, where n is the sample size.

Gradient:

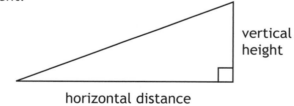

$$\text{gradient} = \frac{\text{vertical height}}{\text{horizontal distance}}$$

MARKS | DO NOT WRITE IN THIS MARGIN

Total marks — 55

Attempt ALL questions

1. Publicity material is to be designed for a theatre show that is being sponsored by a local company.

   All the publicity material must feature the company logo.

   The company logo is in the shape of a triangle.

   The designer is to produce a small "flyer" and a large poster.

   The designer produces a sketch for the flyer as shown.

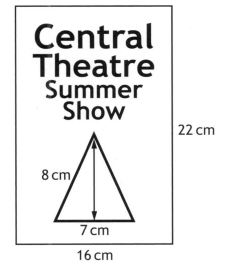

   (a) The ratio of the dimensions in the poster to those in the flyer is 7:2.

   Calculate the dimensions of the logo as it will appear on the poster.   **2**

   (b) The design brief specifies that the company logo must be between 9% and 12% of the area of any publicity material.

   Does this design fit these specifications?   **4**

[Turn over

MARKS DO NOT WRITE IN THIS MARGIN

2. Patryk is a keen cyclist.

Before Patryk goes for a cycle he checks the recommended air pressure for his tyres using the graph below.

Patryk weighs 73 kilograms and he is using 700 × 23C tyres.

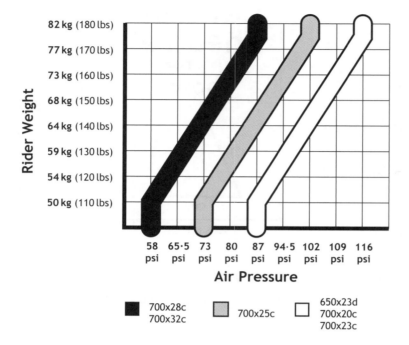

The gauge below shows the reading when he checks his front tyre.

(a) State any adjustment Patryk should make so that his tyre has the correct air pressure.

3

MARKS | DO NOT WRITE IN THIS MARGIN

2. **(continued)**

Patryk has a bicycle trip computer.

To calibrate the computer he must enter the circumference of the front tyre of his bicycle.

The diameter of the rim is 622 millimetres and the depth of the tyre is 23 millimetres as shown in the diagram below.

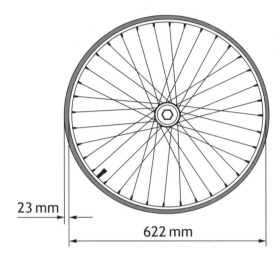

(b) What value should Patryk enter into his bicycle trip computer?

Round your answer to the nearest millimetre.　　　　　　　　　　**3**

[Turn over

MARKS DO NOT WRITE IN THIS MARGIN

3. Mrs Smith has decided to get the roof of her extension re-slated.

She contacts a local roofing contractor to get an estimate.

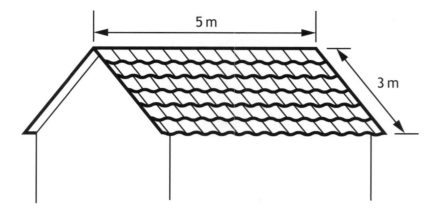

Each side of the roof has dimensions 5 m by 3 m as shown.

The builder gives her a quote for the replacement slates.

He uses the following method to work out his estimate:

- calculate the area of one side

- double this (total area)

- double again (overlapping slates)

- multiply by 16 (to get the number of slates required)

- add on 15% (for cuts and breakages).

The cost of each slate is 97 pence.

He rounds his estimate to the nearest hundred pounds.

The builder tells Mrs Smith he will "throw in" any additional materials for free.

(a) How much is the estimate for replacement slates?   3

3. (continued)

Mrs Smith asks for a total price including labour.

The builder works this out using the following:

Strip and clean roof — 8 hours

Replace slates — 1 square metre/ hour

Rate — £22 per hour.

(b) How much will the labour costs be?

2

(c) Mrs Smith will go ahead with the work if the written estimate is less than £2,500.

Complete the written estimate below.

Written Estimate

Client	Mrs Smith
Estimated cost of slates	£
Labour Costs	£
Sub-total	£
VAT at 20%	£
TOTAL COST	£

Will Mrs Smith accept the builder's estimate?

2

[Turn over

MARKS

4. A seaplane flies from an airport on a bearing of 050° at a speed of 170 mph for 36 minutes.

It then turns onto a new bearing of 190° and flies at the same speed for a further 1 hour 12 minutes.

(a) Construct a scale drawing to illustrate this journey.

Use a scale of 1 cm:20 miles

4

Airport

4.   **(continued)**

The seaplane continues at the same speed back to the airport.

(b) Use the scale drawing to determine the distance and bearing of the airport from the seaplane.

2

The seaplane burns fuel at 32 litres per hour.

Aviation fuel costs £2·04 per litre.

(c) Calculate the cost of the fuel for the complete journey.

4

[Turn over

MARKS | DO NOT WRITE IN THIS MARGIN

5. The local youth club runs a weekly tuck shop. Any profit that is made is donated to a local charity.

The stem and leaf diagram shows their weekly takings for the first 6 months of this year.

```
0 | 5  7  7  8  9  9
1 | 0  2  5  6  6  7  8  8  8  9
2 | 0  1  1  2  3  5
3 | 0  4
```

n = 24   3 | 4 represents £34

(a) (i) State:

the median

the lower quartile

the upper quartile.   2

(ii) Using the above data construct a boxplot in the space provided.

(An additional diagram, if required, can be found on *Page fourteen*)   2

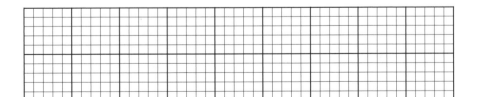

5. **(continued)**

MARKS | DO NOT WRITE IN THIS MARGIN

(b) The monthly profits, in pounds, for the second 6 months of this year, are recorded below.

22   16   25   19   18   20

Calculate:

   (i) the mean monthly profit.   **1**

   (ii) the standard deviation.

      Round your answer to the nearest penny.   **3**

(c) The mean profit and standard deviation, for the same period, the previous year was £16·25 and £2·40 respectively.

Make two valid comparisons between these.   **2**

(d) The local youth club thinks that the mean donations have increased by 25%.

Are they correct?   **2**

[Turn over

MARKS | DO NOT WRITE IN THIS MARGIN

6. In a diving competition there are seven judges.

Each judge gives the diver a raw score out of 10.

Each dive has a difficulty rating.

A rule is then applied which calculates the diver's final score.

The rule is:

- discard the lowest and highest raw scores

- work out the mean of the remaining raw scores

- multiply the mean by 3/5

- multiply this value by the difficulty rating

- round to 1 decimal place.

The table shows the judges' raw scores for two competitors.

Diver	Difficulty rating	Judges' raw scores						
		1	2	3	4	5	6	7
Cheryl	3·2	9·0	9·5	9·0	8·5	7·5	8·5	8·0
Ha-lin	3·5	8·5	7·0	7·5	8·5	8·0	7·5	9·0

(a) In this round, Ha-lin's final score is 16·8.

Is this higher or lower than Cheryl's final score?   4

(b) Cheryl will win the competition if she achieves a final score of 16·9 in her last dive.

(i) If she maintains her mean score from part (a), what is the minimum level of difficulty of dive Cheryl would need to win the competition?   3

MARKS | DO NOT WRITE IN THIS MARGIN

6 **(b)** **(continued)**

(ii) If Cheryl chooses a dive with a difficulty rating of 3·4, what mean score would she need to receive from the judges to win the competition?

3

(c) Regulations state that a 10 metre high diving platform must be:

- 6 m in length
- 3 m in width
- 0·25 m deep at front edge, and 0·5 m at back edge
- made of concrete.

The diagram shows one such platform.

Will 7 m³ of concrete be enough to build the platform?

4

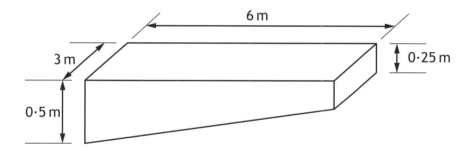

[END OF QUESTION PAPER]

ADDITIONAL SPACE FOR ANSWERS

Additional Diagram for Question 5(a)

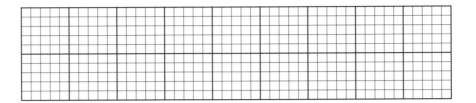

MARKS DO NOT WRITE IN THIS MARGIN

ADDITIONAL SPACE FOR ANSWERS

[BLANK PAGE]

DO NOT WRITE ON THIS PAGE

NATIONAL 5

2016

N5

National Qualifications 2016

Mark

X744/75/01

**Lifeskills Mathematics
Paper 1 (Non-Calculator)**

WEDNESDAY, 4 MAY

9:00 AM — 9:50 AM

Fill in these boxes and read what is printed below.

Full name of centre

Town

Forename(s)

Surname

Number of seat

Date of birth

Day	Month	Year

Scottish candidate number

Total marks — 35

Attempt ALL questions.

You may NOT use a calculator.

Full credit will be given only to solutions which contain appropriate working.

State the units for your answer where appropriate.

Write your answers clearly in the spaces provided in this booklet. Additional space for answers is provided at the end of this booklet. If you use this space you must clearly identify the question number you are attempting.

Use **blue** or **black** ink.

Before leaving the examination room you must give this booklet to the Invigilator; if you do not, you may lose all the marks for this paper.

FORMULAE LIST

Circumference of a circle: $C = \pi d$

Area of a circle: $A = \pi r^2$

Theorem of Pythagoras:

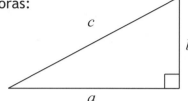

$$a^2 \quad b^2 \quad c^2$$

Volume of a cylinder: $V = \pi r^2 h$

Volume of a prism: $V = Ah$

Volume of a cone: $V = \frac{1}{3}\pi r^2 h$

Volume of a sphere: $V = \frac{4}{3}\pi r^3$

Standard deviation: $s = \sqrt{\dfrac{\Sigma(x-\overline{x})^2}{n-1}} = \sqrt{\dfrac{\Sigma x^2 - (\Sigma x)^2/n}{n-1}}$, where n is the sample size.

Gradient:

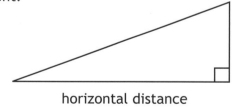

$$\text{gradient} = \frac{\text{vertical height}}{\text{horizontal distance}}$$

MARKS DO NOT WRITE IN THIS MARGIN

Total marks — 35

Attempt ALL questions

1. A restaurant can buy long grain rice in two sizes of bags.

   - A 9 kg bag costs £25·65
   - A 20 kg bag costs £57·20

   Which size of bag is better value for the restaurant?

   Use your working to justify your answer.   **3**

2. Aneesha and Brian are playing a board game. Each move is determined by rolling two dice.

   Aneesha requires a total of **10 or more** on her next roll to win the game.

   What is the probability of Aneesha winning the game on the next roll?

   Give your answer as a fraction.   **3**

   [Turn over

3. Gary lives in Biggar and has to go to a meeting in Edinburgh.

He plans to travel to his meeting by bus.

He uses this bus timetable to plan his journey.

Dumfries ● Biggar ● Edinburgh

Monday to Friday

Route Number	101	101	101	101	101	102	101	101	101	101	101	102
Dumfries Whitesands Stance 4		0535	0710		0910	1025			1315			1815
Heathhall		0543	0720		0920	|			1325			|
Amisfield Main Rd		0547	0725		0925	|			1330			|
Parkgate		0552	0730		0930	|			1335			|
St Ann's		0557	0736		0936	|			1341			|
Beattock Primary School		0606	0745		0945	|			1350			|
Moffat High St Stance 2		0612	0752		0952	|			1357			|
Holywood		|	|		|	1031			|			1821
Auldgirth		|	|		|	1039			|			1829
Closeburn		|	|		|	1046			|			1836
Thornhill Cross		|	|		|	1050			|			1840
Durisdeermill		|	|		|	1100			|			1850
Troloss		|	|		|	1105			|			1855
Elvanfoot		|	|		|	1117			|			1907
Crawford		0633	0813		1013	1128			1418			1913
Abington Village		0640	0820		1020	1135			1425			1920
Abington Service Area		0646	0827		1027	1142			1432			1927
Roberton		0651	0832		1032	1147			1437			1932
Lamington		0657	0838		1038	1153			1443			1938
Coulter		0702	0843		1043	1158			1448			1943
Biggar	0633	0709	0853	0953	1053	1208	1253	1353	1458	1623	1803	1953
Dolphinton	0644	0721	0905	1004	1104	1219	1304	1404	1509	1634	1814	2004
West Linton	0651	0731	0915	1011	1111	1226	1311	1411	1516	1641	1821	2011
Carlops	0655	0735	0920	1015	1115	1230	1315	1415	1520	1645	1825	2015
Silverburn	0702	0741	0927	1021	1121	1236	1321	1421	1526	1651	1831	2021
Penicuik Town Centre Stop C	0707	|	0932	1026	|	1241	1326	1426	|	1656	1836	2026
Flotterstone	0717	0746	0942	1036	1126	1251	1336	1436	1531	1706	1846	2034
Fairmilehead, Swanston Drive	0724	0753	0948	1042	1132	1257	1342	1442	1537	1712	1852	2039
Morningside Station	0732	0801	0956	1050	1140	1305	1350	1450	1545	1720	1900	2045
Tollcross	0740	0809	1004	1058	1148	1313	1358	1458	1553	1728	1908	2050
Lothian Road, Caledonian Hotel	0749	0818	1011	1104	1154	1319	1404	1504	1600	1735	1914	2055
Edinburgh Bus Stance E	0801	0830	1021	1114	1204	1329	1414	1514	1611	1745	1924	2102

His meeting in Edinburgh starts at 11:30 am.

It will take him 25 minutes to walk from the Edinburgh bus stance to his meeting.

What is the latest bus he can catch in Biggar to be at his meeting on time?　　2

MARKS | DO NOT WRITE IN THIS MARGIN

4. Seonaid is saving up to buy a tablet computer costing £388.

   She earns £7·30 per hour and works for 30 hours each week.

   Seonaid is paid at the end of each week.

   She pays £5·32 in Income Tax and £7·68 in National Insurance each week.

   Her living expenses are £86 per week.

   Seonaid saves **half** of the money that she has left each week towards the tablet computer.

   How many weeks will it take her to save up enough money to buy the computer?   **3**

[Turn over

MARKS | DO NOT WRITE IN THIS MARGIN

5. A computer company is researching how long it would take to develop a new games console and bring it to market.

The following table of necessary tasks was produced.

Activity	Description	Preceding Task	Time (months)
A	Product design	None	12
B	Market research	None	2
C	Production analysis	A	3
D	Product model	A	4
E	Sales brochure	A	1
F	Product testing	D	5
G	Cost analysis	C	3
H	Sales training	B,E	2
I	Pricing	H	1
J	Project report	F,G,I	1

(a) Complete the diagram below to show the tasks and times in the boxes. (An additional diagram, if required, can be found on *Page twelve*). **2**

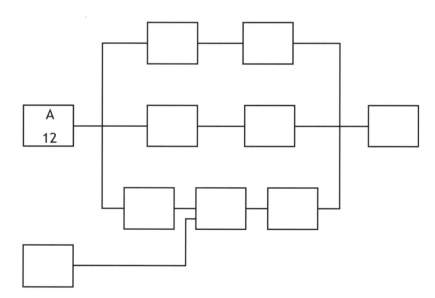

(b) The company want this entire process to be completed in 2 years.

Based on the times given, is this possible?

Show working to justify your answer. **2**

MARKS | DO NOT WRITE IN THIS MARGIN

6. A farmer needs to **completely enclose** this field with a new fence.

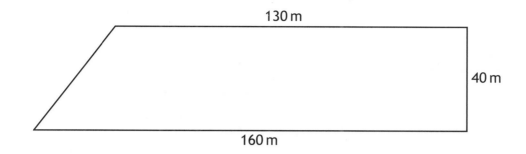

130 m

40 m

160 m

The fence is only sold in 80 metre rolls.

Each roll costs £73·99.

Calculate the cost of the new fence. **5**

[Turn over

7. The table below shows the vehicle tax to be paid on different vehicles.

The amount of vehicle tax paid depends on the CO_2 emissions of the vehicle and the fuel type.

Standard Rates – The following table contains the rates of vehicle tax for already registered cars, based on CO_2 emissions and fuel type.

| | | Petrol Car (Tax Class 48) and Diesel Car (Tax Class 49) | | | | |
| | | Non Direct Debit | | Direct Debit | | |
Bands	CO_2 emission figure (g/km)	12 months	Six months	Single 12 month payment	Total payable by 12 monthly instalments	Single six month payment
Band A	Up to 100	£0	-	-	-	-
Band B	101 to 110	£20	-	£20	£21	-
Band C	111 to 120	£30	-	£30	£31·50	-
Band D	121 to 130	£110	£60·50	£110	£115·50	£57·75
Band E	131 to 140	£130	£71·50	£130	£136·50	£68·25
Band F	141 to 150	£145	£79·75	£145	£152·25	£76·13
Band G	151 to 165	£180	£99	£180	£189	£94·50
Band H	166 to 175	£205	£112·75	£205	£215·25	£107·63
Band I	176 to 185	£225	£123·75	£225	£236·25	£118·13
Band J	186 to 200	£265	£145·75	£265	£278·25	£139·13
Band K	201 to 225	£290	£159·50	£290	£304·50	£152·25
Band L	226 to 255	£490	£269·50	£490	£514·50	£257·25
Band M	Over 255	£505	£277·75	£505	£530·25	£265·13

Tom buys a **petrol** car which has a CO_2 emission figure of 142 g/km.

Tom decides to pay his vehicle tax by direct debit in two single six month payments.

How much more expensive is this than a single 12 month payment by direct debit?

3

8. A new playground is planned for Aberbeath Primary School.

It will be a rectangle measuring 19 metres by 8 metres.

A semi-circular sandpit will be built within the playground as shown

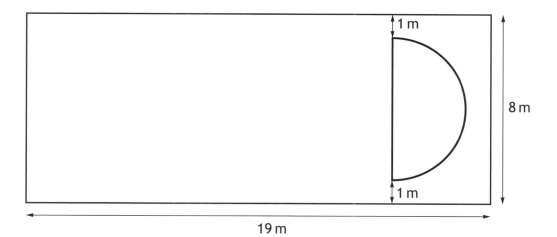

The playground, excluding the sandpit, is to be covered in rubber tiles.

Calculate the area to be covered by the rubber tiles.

Take $\pi = 3 \cdot 14$.

Give your answer to **3 significant figures**.

4

[Turn over

MARKS | DO NOT WRITE IN THIS MARGIN

9. A picture is glued onto a piece of card as shown.

- The picture is a rectangle with dimensions 4 cm by 5 cm.
- The rectangular card has an **area** 2·8 times greater than the **area** of the picture.
- One of the dimensions of the piece of card is 7 cm.

Calculate the other dimension of the piece of card. 3

MARKS | DO NOT WRITE IN THIS MARGIN

10. Bradley decides to cycle from Kilsyth to the highest point of Tak-Ma-Doon Road.

   • The horizontal distance between these two places is 4·5 kilometres.

   • Kilsyth is 70 metres above sea level.

   • The highest point of Tak-Ma-Doon Road is 320 metres above sea level.

   (a) Calculate the average gradient between Kilsyth and the highest point of Tak-Ma-Doon Road.

   Give your answer as a fraction **in its simplest form**.   3

   (b) One part of the road has gradient $\frac{2}{25}$.
   Is this steeper than the average gradient?
   You must justify your answer.   2

[END OF QUESTION PAPER]

ADDITIONAL SPACE FOR ANSWERS

Additional diagram for Question 5 (a)

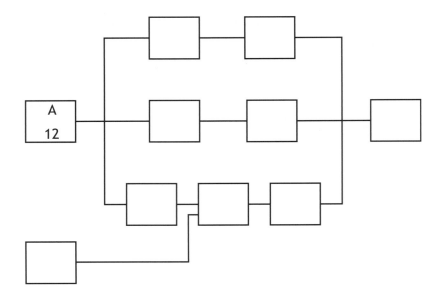

MARKS | DO NOT WRITE IN THIS MARGIN

ADDITIONAL SPACE FOR ANSWERS

Page thirteen

ADDITIONAL SPACE FOR ANSWERS

ADDITIONAL SPACE FOR ANSWERS

MARKS

DO NOT WRITE IN THIS MARGIN

ADDITIONAL SPACE FOR ANSWERS

FOR OFFICIAL USE

N5

National Qualifications 2016

Mark

X744/75/02

Lifeskills Mathematics Paper 2

WEDNESDAY, 4 MAY

10:10 AM — 11:50 AM

Fill in these boxes and read what is printed below.

Full name of centre

Town

Forename(s)

Surname

Number of seat

Date of birth

Day	Month	Year

Scottish candidate number

Total marks — 55

Attempt ALL questions.

You may use a calculator.

Full credit will be given only to solutions which contain appropriate working.

State the units for your answer where appropriate.

Write your answers clearly in the spaces provided in this booklet. Additional space for answers is provided at the end of this booklet. If you use this space you must clearly identify the question number you are attempting.

Use **blue** or **black** ink.

Before leaving the examination room you must give this book to the Invigilator; if you do not, you may lose all the marks for this paper.

FORMULAE LIST

Circumference of a circle: $C = \pi d$

Area of a circle: $A = \pi r^2$

Theorem of Pythagoras:

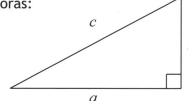

$$a^2 \quad b^2 \quad c^2$$

Volume of a cylinder: $V = \pi r^2 h$

Volume of a prism: $V = Ah$

Volume of a cone: $V = \frac{1}{3}\pi r^2 h$

Volume of a sphere: $V = \frac{4}{3}\pi r^3$

Standard deviation: $s = \sqrt{\dfrac{\Sigma(x - \bar{x})^2}{n-1}} = \sqrt{\dfrac{\Sigma x^2 - (\Sigma x)^2/n}{n-1}}$, where n is the sample size.

Gradient:

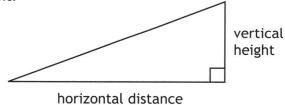

$$\text{gradient} = \frac{\text{vertical height}}{\text{horizontal distance}}$$

MARKS | DO NOT WRITE IN THIS MARGIN

Total marks — 55

Attempt ALL questions

1. The population of Scotland is recorded to the nearest hundred.

   In 2014, the population was 5 347 600.

   In 2015, the population was 5 369 000.

   (a) Show that the percentage growth in population from 2014 to 2015 was 0·4%.   **2**

   (b) If the population continues to grow at the same rate, calculate the expected population in 2018.

   Give your answer to the **nearest hundred**.   **3**

[Turn over

MARKS

2. Chris flew from Perth, Australia, to London, United Kingdom, on Saturday 9th January 2016.

   - The plane left Perth, Australia, at 13:05.

   - The total journey time, including a stopover in Dubai, is 20 hours and 25 minutes.

   - Perth time is 8 hours ahead of London.

   At what time did the plane land in London?   **2**

MARKS | DO NOT WRITE IN THIS MARGIN

3. In September 2014 there was a referendum to determine the future of Scotland.

An opinion poll was taken in December 2013.
The question asked was "Should Scotland be an independent country?"

The results are shown in the pie chart below.

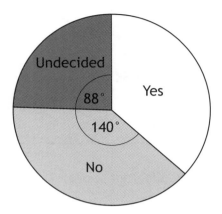

Another opinion poll was taken in April 2014.
1208 people were asked the same question as in December 2013.

The results of this poll are shown in the table below.

YES	NO	UNDECIDED
447	616	145

Compare the two opinion polls and make one relevant comment on the differences between them.

3

[Turn over

MARKS | DO NOT WRITE IN THIS MARGIN

4. Alison and Michael are travelling to Inverie on Knoydart for a holiday. They must take a ferry from Mallaig to Inverie

(a) The direct distance from Mallaig to Inverie is 9·8 kilometres.

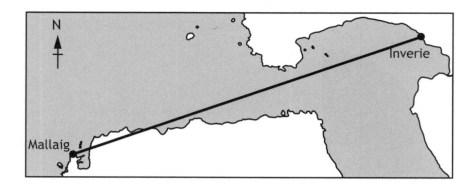

(i) Calculate the scale used in the diagram above.   1

(ii)

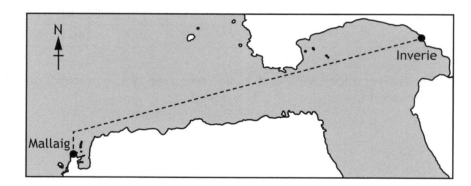

The ferry leaves Mallaig and travels North for 0·6 km.

The ferry then changes direction to sail directly to Inverie.

Use the second diagram to find the bearing and distance, in kilometres, that the ferry must travel on the **second part** of its journey.   2

MARKS

4. **(continued)**

(b) The average speed of the ferry from Mallaig to Inverie is
24 ± 3 kilometres per hour depending on tide and weather.

What is the shortest time that the **complete** ferry journey might take?

Give your answer to the **nearest minute**.

3

[Turn over

5. Fiona is planning to stay in New York, USA, for three days.
She researches the cost of various attractions.

Attraction	Full price in US Dollars
Empire State Building	$32
Top of the Rock Observation Deck	$30
Statue of Liberty Cruise	$40
9/11 Memorial and Museum	$24
Waxworks	$37
One World Observatory	$32

Fiona will visit all six of these attractions while she is there.

Fiona plans to buy a discount card to reduce the cost of visiting these attractions.

Not all of the attractions are included in all of the cards. Fiona must pay full price for these.

Card 1: NY Card

NY Card

Attractions:

★ Sea and Space Museum ★   ★ Top of the Rock Observation Deck ★

★ Museum of Natural History ★   ★ 9/11 Memorial and Museum ★

★ Statue of Liberty Cruise ★   ★ Empire State Building ★

★★★★ Total Cost $114 ★★★★

Benefits:

These six attractions can be visited for a single payment of $114.
This card can only be used once per attraction.
It is valid for 30 days from first use.

Card 2: Explore NY Card

Explore NY Card
Attractions:

9/11 Memorial and Museum · Statue of Liberty Cruise

Museum of Natural History · Sea and Space Museum

Empire State Building · Top of the Rock Observation Deck

Waxworks · Carnegie Hall · Rockefeller Centre Tour

Cost for any 3 attractions $71

Benefits:

This card can be used for any 3 attractions from the list.
This card can only be used once per attraction.
It is valid for 30 days from first use.

MARKS DO NOT WRITE IN THIS MARGIN

5. (continued)

Card 3: NY Town Pass

NY Town Pass

80+ attractions are included for one price.
When activated the card is valid for 1, 2, 3 or 5 days.
These must be consecutive days.

Cost

$90 1 day pass $180 3 day pass
$140 2 day pass $190 5 day pass

Benefits:

All of Fiona's chosen attractions can be visited with this card.

(a) During her three-day visit, Fiona will visit two attractions each day.

Fiona is going to buy one discount card.

(i) Calculate the total cost of all six attractions if Fiona buys Card 1.   **2**

(ii) Calculate the cheapest price that Fiona could pay for entry to her six chosen attractions.   **4**

(b) Fiona pays the cheapest price for entry to her six chosen attractions.

She pays before leaving the UK.

The cost is £100·96.

Calculate the exchange rate that Fiona received.

Give your answer correct to **3 decimal places**.   **2**

[Turn over

MARKS | DO NOT WRITE IN THIS MARGIN

6. Fraser tests motorcycle tyres on racing circuits.

On Monday he tested Goodhold tyres.

His lap times, in seconds, are given below.

    81·8   81·7   81·6   81·0   80·3   80·2

(a) For Fraser's times on Goodhold tyres, calculate:

    (i) the mean;   1

    (ii) the standard deviation.   3

MARKS | DO NOT WRITE IN THIS MARGIN

6.   (continued)

(b)   Fraser then changed to Megagrip tyres and recorded his times for another six laps.

These times produced a mean of 81·6 seconds and standard deviation of 0·65 seconds.

Make two valid comments comparing the two types of tyres.

2

(c)   Another rider completed one lap of the circuit in 81·0 seconds.

The track is 3·6 kilometres long.

Calculate his average speed in **kilometres per hour**.

3

[Turn over

MARKS | DO NOT WRITE IN THIS MARGIN

7. Grace works for a company selling fitted kitchens.

   She is paid a basic monthly salary of £500.

   She also receives 5% commission on all her sales **above** £8000.

   In January Grace sells £23 000 of goods.

   Her monthly deductions are 12% of her gross income.

   Grace writes down her budget for the month.

Rent	£245
Bills	£198
Food	£164
Entertaining	£75

   Grace saves any surplus.

   (a) Calculate Grace's **net** pay for January.   4

   (b) (i) Calculate the surplus that Grace will have for January.   1

   (ii) Grace's rent increases to £260 per month.

   Calculate the percentage increase in her rent.   2

7. **(continued)**

(c) To buy a car Grace needs to borrow £4500.

She wants to repay the loan **as soon as possible**.

She investigates the cost of the loan from five different lenders.

The table shows the repayments for a £4500 loan.

Lender	12 months	24 months	36 months
Tasko	£413·86	£215·07	£150·60
Bank of Shapes	£418·54	£219·31	£157·42
TMS	£458·83	£260·59	£197·74
Premier Bank	£422·46	£214·74	£159·21
Free Bank	£432·99	£234·15	£170·09

Grace assumes that she will earn the same commission each month.

Calculate her **new monthly surplus** and determine from which lender she should take her loan, and over how many months.

2

[Turn over

MARKS | DO NOT WRITE IN THIS MARGIN

8. Brendan makes candles from blocks of wax.

   Each block of wax is a cuboid measuring 30 cm by 20 cm by 20 cm as shown.

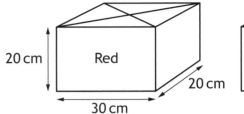 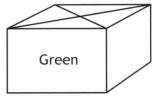 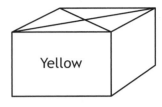

Red   Green   Yellow

20 cm   20 cm   30 cm

Each candle contains the colours red, green and yellow in the ratio 3 : 1 : 2 respectively.

Each candle is a cube with volume 729 cm^3.

(a) Brendan only has 1 block of each colour.
   What is the maximum number of candles that he can make?   **3**

Brendan makes the maximum number of candles.
Any wax that is left over is thrown away.

Each block of wax costs £13·75.
Brendan also buys wicks which cost 18p per candle.

Brendan adds 65% to his costs when calculating the selling price of each candle.

(b) What is Brendan's selling price for each candle?   **3**

MARKS | DO NOT WRITE IN THIS MARGIN

8. (continued)

Brendan also makes blue candles in the shape of a cylinder with a cone on top as shown.

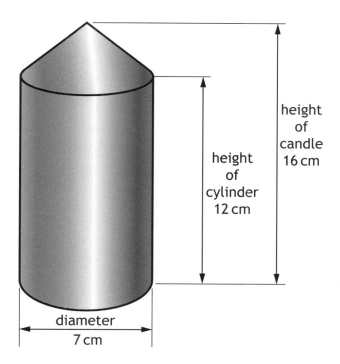

height of candle 16 cm

height of cylinder 12 cm

diameter 7 cm

(c) He buys blue wax in blocks with volume 12 000 cm³.

Brendan thinks that he can make 25 of these candles from one block of wax.

Is he correct?

Use your working to justify your answer.   7

[END OF QUESTION PAPER]

MARKS | DO NOT WRITE IN THIS MARGIN

ADDITIONAL SPACE FOR ANSWERS

MARKS | DO NOT WRITE IN THIS MARGIN

ADDITIONAL SPACE FOR ANSWERS

Page seventeen

MARKS | DO NOT WRITE IN THIS MARGIN

ADDITIONAL SPACE FOR ANSWERS

MARKS | DO NOT WRITE IN THIS MARGIN

ADDITIONAL SPACE FOR ANSWERS

ADDITIONAL SPACE FOR ANSWERS

NATIONAL 5

Answers

NATIONAL 5 LIFESKILLS MATHEMATICS 2014

Paper 1

1. $\frac{1}{10}$

2. No, Frances is not in good health as her temperature (37.7°C) is above the upper tolerance (37.2°C) of good health

3. (a) 5 (m)

   (b) 21 m²

4. (a) £259

   (b) Yes he can afford the holiday as he can save £52 more than he needs

5. 8200 metres (8·2 km)

6. (a) Task letters and times inserted in chart

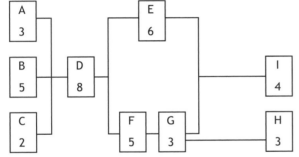

   (b) No, because it will take 25 hours

7. (a) Boys with valid reason

   (b) 26, 18, 30

   (c)

   10   18   26   30   42

8. (a) NOK 6000

   (b) £87·50

9. Proof

Paper 2

1. (£)30, (£)9·30

2. (a) Monthy Deal 1 is cheaper

   (b) £42·19 (accept £42.18)

3. (a) Mark position

   (b) (i) Mark position
       (ii) 340km, 200°

4. (a) £135 000

   (b) No, value of Saraish's house is about £1000 lower

5. (a) 9·8 metres

   (b) £254·15

6. (a) 0·9s

   (b) 179 (km/hr)

   (c) 1 hour 47 minutes 8·8 seconds

7. (a) £968·40, £357·48, £741·82

   (b) Choice of surface plus reason eg, slabs cheapest per year, or gravel cheaper initially etc

NATIONAL 5 LIFESKILLS MATHEMATICS 2015

Paper 1

1. No, as 105 < 110

2. 0310 / 3·10 am

3.

Shelf 1	A, D or F
Shelf 2	B, G, F or D
Shelf 3	C, E
Shelf 4	H, K
Shelf 5	I, J, L

4. No, as 85% < 88%

5. £2(·00) / 200p per litre

6. £163·75

7. Yes, since 3·5m > 320cm

8. **Rule 1:** Yes, as 640 is upper limit of tolerance
   Rule 2: No, as 17/30 > 1/2

9. (a) £360
   (b) £165·50

10. (a) 237·12m^2
   (b) £4077

Paper 2

1. (a) Dimensions are 24·5cm and 28cm
   (b) No, logo is (7%) 8% which is less than lower limit of 9%

2. (a) Add 4 (psi) or lose 5kg in weight **or** add more air so it reads 109psi
   (b) 2099 (mm)

3. (a) £1100
   (b) £836
   (c) Yes, supported by working, ie

Slates	1100
Labour	836
Sub-total	1936
VAT	387·20
Total	2323·20

4. (a) Route correctly drawn
   (b) 342°, 142 miles
   (c) £172·03

5. (a) (i) Q_2 = (£)17·50,
       Q_1 = (£)9·50, Q_3 = (£)21
   (ii) Boxplot drawn correctly showing 5-figure summary
   (b) (i) $\bar{x}$ = (£)20
   (ii) s = (£)3·16
   (c) 2 valid comments, eg 'On average there is more profit being made this year'; 'There is more variation in profit this year'
   (d) No, as 23% < 25%

6. (a) It is higher (16·8>16·5)
   (b) (i) 3·3
   (ii) 8·3
   (c) Yes, as 7 > 6·75

NATIONAL 5 LIFESKILLS MATHEMATICS 2016

Paper 1

1. 9 kg bag, supported by working

2. $\dfrac{6}{36}\left(\dfrac{1}{6}\right)$

3. 0853 (from Biggar)

4. 7 weeks

5. (a) Task letters and times inserted correctly, ie

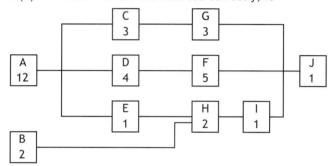

   (b) Yes, as it takes 22 months

6. (£)369·95

7. (£)7·26

8. 138 m^2

9. 8 (cm)

10. (a) $\dfrac{1}{18}$
   (b) Yes, $\dfrac{2}{25} > \dfrac{2}{36}$

Paper 2

1. (a) Proof, e.g. $\dfrac{21400}{5347600} \times 100 = 0.4$
       or 5347600 ÷ 100 × 0·4 + 5347600 = 5369000
   (b) 5 433 700

2. 01:30 (on Sunday 10th)

3. Make one valid comment, eg similar proportion chose 'yes' in survey 2; larger proportion chose 'no' in survey 2; smaller proportion chose 'undecided' in survey 2

4. (a) (i) 1:100 000
   (ii) 074°, 9·6 km
   (b) 23 (minutes)

5. (a) (i) ($)183
   (ii) ($)157 supported by working
   (b) £1 gives $1·555 or $1 gives £0·643

6. (a) (i) 81·1
   (ii) 0·72
   (b) Two valid comments, eg on average Goodhold give a faster lap time; lap times with Goodhold are less consistent
   (c) 160 (km/hr)

7. (a) (£)1100

   (b) (i) (£)418

      (ii) 6·1(%)

   (c) Premier bank, 24 months

8. (a) 32 candles

   (b) (£)2·43 or 2·42

   (c) No, he can't make 25 candles, supported by working

Acknowledgements

Permission has been sought from all relevant copyright holders and Hodder Gibson is grateful for the use of the following:

Image © cobalt88/Shutterstock.com (2014 Paper 2 page 3);
Image © hamurishi/Shutterstock.com (2014 Paper 2 page 4);
Image © Photoseeker/Shutterstock.com (2014 Paper 2 page 4);
Image © Aaron Amat/Shutterstock.com (2014 Paper 2 page 4);
Image © nito/Shutterstock.com (2014 Paper 2 page 4);
Image © Coprid/Shutterstock.com (2015 Paper 1 page 5);
An image of a timetable adapted from 'Stagecoach Dumfries – Edinburgh Bus Timetable' © Stagecoach Group (2016 Paper 1 page 4);
Image © MiloVad/Shutterstock.com (2016 Paper 2 page 10).